Health Care; God's Plan

Health Care; God's Plan

Kenneth G. Morris

Empowered Publications Inc.
Millry, Alabama
www.empoweredpublicationsinc.com

© 1994 Kenneth G. Morris

All Rights Reserved.

Cover Design by Christian Author Partner

All scripture texts are taken from the King James Version.

Empowered Publications Inc.
529 County Road 31
Millry, Alabama 36558
www.empoweredpublicationsinc.com

ISBN: 978-1-943033-11-9

From the Editor,

This book was written and originally published prior to the passing of Obama Care, and our nation's current health care crisis. It is uncanny how a man of God had the foresight to pen this book. However, the church should never be taken unaware of the world's devices. Instead, the church should be ready to combat the attacks of the enemy on every front, including the land of politics.

This time of turmoil has created a great opportunity for the church to be the vessel that God intended. It is past time for the church to rise up, and be the help that the world needs.

We, the church, have the answer to this world's problems. Sickness, disease, addictions, and brokeness can all be restored with one touch of the Master's hand. We are commanded to go into all the world and preach the gospel. The gospel message includes the availability of salvation, and healing for sin-sick souls.

Let us leave off the debate of denominationalism, and get back to our sole purpose. Let us take the good news of healing to this nation. And unto the world.

Yet, before we can instruct others how to receive their healing, we must first learn how to receive this gift for ourselves. The church has many members stricken with cancer. Surprisingly, many are addicted to prescription pills. We need to locate the portal to our Great Physician.

Heath Care; God's Plan maps out the route to divine healing as found in the Word of God. This publication is intended to strengthen your faith, and to place you in a position to receive a miracle in your body or in your soul.

I pray that God will touch your life as He has touched mine as you read these pages.

Table of Contents

Introduction   9

Chapter One   11
    The Need For This Book

Chapter Two   21
    Is Divine Healing A True Bible Doctrine?

Chapter Three   33
    Divine Healing In The New Testament

Chapter Four   45
    Errors Being Taught On Divine Healing
    And Biblical Answers To Them

Chapter Five   55
    Divine Healing For The Individual Person Today

Chapter Six   71
    Not All Are Healed

Chapter Seven   79
    Receiving Divine Healing

Introduction

It is a very strong conviction of mine, that the church of today has allowed the ministry and the practice of divine healing to be stolen away from it, to a large degree. To me, this is a very sad happening. I believe that divine healing is, or at least should be, a vital part of the ministry of the local church.

I acknowledge the fact, sadly, that this ministry has been grossly misused by those who have tried to make profit or gain from it. However, we should not fail in this ministry just because someone misuses it. Telephones are used for the wrong purpose every day, yet we continue to use them.

Another reason for the lack of ministry in the field of divine healing, is that only a few are willing to pay the price for such a ministry.

It is my hope and prayer this text will help those who are sick to be healed, and help others to minister healing to the sick and suffering. I do not claim that this is a complete study, for it is not. My hope and prayer is that after reading through this book and following the instructions of the Word of God, many will receive the blessing of divine healing.

Kenneth G. Morris.

Chapter One

The Need For This Book

BELOVED, I WISH ABOVE ALL THINGS THAT THOU MAYEST PROSPER AND BE IN HEALTH, EVEN AS THY SOUL PROSPERETH. III JOHN 2

The need for this book has been impressed on my mind as the debate over health has become a much talked about political issue. The President has a plan. The Democrats have a plan. And the Republicans also have a plan.

All of these plans have faults and limitations. Even the sponsors and supporters admit to this fact. Short comings and uncertainties hamper the initiation of any of these plans.

Eventually, some sort of socialized health care will become law in this country. No one knows exactly what kind of plan it will be, or how it will affect the citizens of this nation. As we hope for the best, we fear the worse.

With issues such as abortion and euthanasia being debated, as to how they will fit into the plan, it becomes a frightful thing.

The talk of cut-off points in relationship to the age of the individual being treated, and limits on the amount of money that can be spent treating an individual, is disturbing.

A friend of mine, who is a medical doctor, aroused my interest as he told of a friend of his whose father-in-law suffered a broken hip as they were vacationing in a country that has socialized medicine. After much searching and persuading, a hospital was found that would accept him, and a doctor was located who agreed to do the surgery needed to repair this broken hip.

The reluctance and hesitation were caused by the fact that his father-in-law was not covered under the health care plan of that country. He was not a citizen of that country. He had only gone there for a vacation.

After the operation was finished, and the man was recovering, pneumonia set in making him a very sick man. When no treatment was forthcoming, the son-in law questioned hospital personnel as to the reason. The answer he received was stunning.

"Your father-in-law is seventy-five years old. We stop treatment for pneumonia at age seventy."

This man paid an enormous sum of money, chartering a jet, to fly his wife's father home to the United States so he could be treated for this infection.

This is alarming! We may not only see health care limited by the amount of money allowed to be spent on a person, or limitations placed on treatment of certain diseases by the age of the person, we may see treatment vary according to the location of the person who is sick and in need of medical aid.

This variation of treatment may not necessarily be from country to country. It could very well be from state to state. There is even a remote possibility that care could vary within a given state. People in rural areas may be subjected to a totally different system than those who live in the cities, and metropolitan areas.

Another thing that causes thoughts to arise in my mind is the talk of assigning families and individuals to certain doctors and health care providers, largely taking from us the freedom to choose our own doctors, hospitals, nursing homes, etc.

I cannot help but believe that many doctors and health care providers will give different treatment to people who come to them because they are assigned to them, than they would if these same people came to them by choice.

What kind of service would we expect to receive if we were assigned to a certain supermarket, or a certain auto service center with no option to go elsewhere, if we were not satisfied with the service rendered to us?

- In emergencies and after hours, will help be readily available?
- Will there be certain times, certain places, and people that one can see for health care?
- What will a person do for health care when the allotted amount of dollars has been spent?
- When a cut off age has been reached?
- When sickness strikes while away from the locale in which one is covered?
- After hours or on holidays when the providers one

is assigned to is out and unable to be seen?

There is another disturbing question that comes to my mind at this point. Since money will play such a factor in universal health care and socialized medicine, when a person is diagnosed with a terminal illness and deemed incurable, what then?

- Will it be looked upon as a waste of money and resources to continue treatment for such a one?
- Will the hopeless be left to die a miserable death?
- Will they be shoved out of the system?
- Will they become a victim of euthanasia, and be put to sleep like a useless animal so that the system will not be overburdened?

The possibility that under a universal plan waiting periods will be initiated is also a matter to be considered. I have read of one country that practices socialized medicine, where the waiting period for cataract surgery is seven months. In many cases, the condition is past help when the waiting period is over. It may be this is the reason for the waiting period.

The last fact we will consider here, but certainly not the least, is the cost factor. Will the average person be able to afford health care?

As these facts are considered, and there are many others that could be considered, the thing that keep going over in my mind is this…?

There Should Be A Better Way

Thank God there is a better way, and this better way is the subject and reason for this book. The better way to health care is God's way.

God was the original health care provider. He was the very first to be mindful of the physical needs of humanity, and He continues to care about the health of mankind.

When we look at the human anatomy, and see the manner in which God created man, we cannot help but to be aware that He cares for our physical health. Proofs that our creator was and is mindful of our physical wellbeing are:
- our vital organs are protected by our skeletal system
- eyelids to protect our eyes
- a warning system known to us a pain
- a reflex system that enables us to move fast, without thought

In the Garden of Eden after the fall, God made coats of skin for Adam and Eve to protect their bodies from the elements of nature.

No Discredit Intended

This book is in no way intended to discredit the many health care professionals who have been a tremendous help and blessing to us for many years. Many of these are equally apprehensive as they await the outcome of the health care debate. They do not know whether they will be allowed to continue their private practice, or whether they will become an employee of the federal government. Along with the rest of us they must wait and see.

While giving credit to good doctors and nurses, the aim of this book is to give hope to many—who are at this point—worried about continuing health care.

I pray that it does not happen, but if we should see the total collapse of the health care system as we now know it, we would not be without hope. We will still have the first, the best, and the most complete and comprehensive health care available to us.

Divine health care cannot be regulated by kings, prime ministers, or presidents. Congresses, courts, or councils cannot affect Gods ways, times, or methods of health care. Divine health care is only affected by the sovereign will of God and the relationship between God and the person or persons who are in need themselves, or who are reaching out to help someone else who is in need.

Some Comparisons

Let's compare the universal health care system, now being debated, with the Divine Health Care Plan, that is the subject of this text.

On the subject of abortion and euthanasia, under the socialized plan, some human decides whether a person should live or die. In many cases, this decision is made for the convenience of another individual, or individuals other than the one who is losing his or her life. This can be nothing but murder.

The giver of life determines the beginning and the end of life under God's plan. "The Lord giveth and the Lord taketh away." There is no selfish motive here. Divine knowledge and wisdom, with an understanding of all tomorrows is brought into focus. Life is started and stopped accordingly.

There is no cut-off point with God in relationship to age or money. Moses was one-hundred-twenty years old at the time of his death. We are told in scripture that "his eye was not dim, nor his natural force abated." There had been no cut-off age with this great man of God. Money doesn't figure in the equation of Divine Health Care. The prophet Isaiah tells us to "buy wine and milk without money and without price." A lame man was healed of his lameness, walked and leaped, and praised God in a situation where the statement was made, "silver and gold have I none."

Since God is everywhere, the location one is in at the time of need makes no difference. There are no after hours or holidays with God. He is always available. God even makes house calls.

The diagnostic systems that determine the problem and the cause of the problem being used by the two systems being discussed here are vastly different. The medical profession of today has many sophisticated tests by which they make diagnosis. Most of the time the tests give accurate information, allowing the physician to come to the right conclusion. There are times, however, when mistakes are made. These mistakes may be due to mechanical malfunction, human error, or a variety of other things. An error in diagnosis may lead to wrong treatment, resulting not only in the person failing to recover, but may also lead to worse things.

God's diagnosis is always true and right. He is all knowing. He knows the end from the beginning. He knows the number of hairs on each head. He knows our need even "before we pray."

A Source Of Great Joy

What a joy! What a comfort! What peace to know that no matter what happens in the health care arena, if we are cut off for one reason or the other, if health care for us and our families is limited by the system, we still have a God who proclaimed, "I am the Lord that healeth thee."

Divine healing and divine health care is no mystical, magical, imaginary thing of the mind. It is real. It is...
- as real as day and night
- as real as the sun and the moon
- as real as life and death
- as real as God Himself.

Many are the testimonies of men and women who have been miraculously healed by the divine power of God. Many are the people alive today, myself included, who are walking, living examples of what is being talked about here, and will be discussed further and in greater detail in the remaining chapters of this work.

Some Good Advice

It is time to think about our personal relationship with God. This is especially true as we consider that healing is the "children's bread."

That we will have to depend more on God now for our physical needs, as well as our spiritual one, is very evident. We must not allow anything to come between us and God. Sin must be dealt with and removed from our hearts, as sin will separate us from God and His power. In the Book of Jeremiah, during a time of trouble, the

Prophet declared to the people of Israel, "Your iniquities have turned away these things, and your sins have withholden good things from you." We must not permit ourselves to live in a way that the good things of God are kept from us.

If the federal government—through its program of socialized medicine—takes from us health care and medical attention as we know it now, if sin and iniquity separates us from God and His divine healing power, then there will be nowhere else to turn.

Think about that for a moment.

Where will this leave individuals, their families, and loved ones? I tell you it will leave them without hope. If as you read these words, you have no personal lord and savior, then you should read no further until you ask Christ to be merciful to you—a sinner—and come into your heart. If you read these words as a Christian who has grown cold and slack allowing unholy things to come into your life, then before reading on in search of a physical healing, you should pause now and make things right with God. Entering into the remaining chapters of this book with a clean, pure, righteous heart, you can expect a miracle.

Chapter Two

Is Divine Healing A True Bible Doctrine?

IF THOU WILT DILIGENTLY HEARKEN TO THE VOICE OF THE LORD THY GOD, AND WILT DO THAT WHICH IS RIGHT IN HIS SIGHT, AND WILT GIVE EAR TO HIS COMMANDMENTS, AND KEEP ALL HIS STATUTES, I WILL PUT NONE OF THESE DISEASES UPON THEE, WHICH I HAVE BROUGHT UPON THE EGYPTIANS: FOR I AM THE LORD THAT HEALETH THEE. ~ EXODUS 15:26

TWO GREAT PROMISES are provided for us in this wonderful verse we are using as a text for this chapter. The promise of divine health, and the promise of divine healing.

The nation Israel, had not been long departed from the bondage of Egypt, at the time God gave these promises to them. The memory of the terrible diseases with which the Egyptians had been afflicted was still fresh on their minds. They had witnessed a period of awful suffering as the plagues from God came into the lives and homes of the inhabitants of the land of Egypt.

As we look at a list of these ten plagues, we must not only consider the plague itself, but also think of the effects it had, and the many diseases that were caused by them.

1. Water was turned to blood
2. The fish died. The condition the river with the blood and dead fish was such that the Egyptians could not drink the water.
3. Frogs came from all the streams, rivers and ponds. There were frogs in the houses. In the beds. In the ovens and in the kneading troughs.
4. Men and beast became infected with lice.
5. The land was corrupted by flies. Flies were everywhere in Egypt, except in Goshen where the Israelites dwelled.
6. A very bad sickness, called murrain, came on all the cattle, horses, asses, camels, oxen and sheep. Terrible boils and blisters, (blains), were on men and beast.
7. Hail and fire fell on the land.
8. The earth itself could not be seen for the multitude of locust that came, and covered it.
9. For three days a thick darkness covered the land of Egypt. This darkness was so total that none could rise from his place. The children of Israel had light in their dwellings.
10. The last of the plagues was the worse. The

death angel passed through the land, and destroyed the first born in every home where the blood of a lamb had not been placed on the lintel and the two side post of the door.

It is not hard to imagine how the fear of these plagues, with their inherit diseases, was on the minds of the people as they journeyed from Egypt, across the Red Sea, headed for the promised land. Could there be any peace and contentment knowing that such awful things could just as easily come on them as they had come on the Egyptians.

Then came the promise of divine health, and the promise of divine healing. These promises—if the conditions are met—would surely make their journey more enjoyable. Whether or not divine healing is a true Bible doctrine, and to establish the fact that it is, is the theme of this chapter. This verse, with its promises, will help with this task.

From Beginning To End

If a subject has its beginning in the first book of the Bible, and its ending in the last book of the Bible, and this subject is taught and illustrated in every division of scripture as it deals with humanity, we can be sure it is a true Bible doctrine. The doctrine of divine healing for the body is such a subject. We do not teach this truth from an isolated verse or two that has been discovered and uncovered someplace in the scripture. It takes no special revelation of the Spirit, no special teaching or training for one to perceive that the Bible deals with, and teaches healing for the physical body by the divine power of God.

An individual must choose—willfully—to be blinded to truth in order to not to recognize that God cares and provides for the physical needs of people, especially His children.

The question is this; Why would anyone want to be blinded, and deny oneself of the greatest blessing God has provided? Though this is a hard thing to understand, there are those among us who do it.

Just as calamity often turns many hearts to the saving grace of God, it may well be that the coming health care crisis will cause many to examine the scripture again in search of truth concerning this matter. If the search is made with sincerity, and an open heart and mind, God will remove the fleshly scales from the eyes and allow those to grasp the truth and reality of this matter. In coming to the knowledge of this truth, and putting full trust in the power of God to heal, many will avail themselves of the greatest healing power known to man—past, present, and future.

There may come a time when this is the only means of health care available to some individuals. If this happens to any, or if it has already happened to some, don't worry. Don't fret. You are in good hands when you are in the hands of the one who created man in the beginning.

Many have experienced, and many are now experiencing, crisis in their lives. Even without a national health care crisis, they face their personal crisis. An incurable disease, improper diagnosis and treatment, lack of insurance, and numerous other possibilities have created such dilemmas. Their only hope is Christ. We all face such straits at some point in our lives. We are never hopeless. We can always call on the Great Physician—Jesus Christ.

In The Beginning

God—the creator—made provisions for the physical body of man in the very beginning of man's existence. Having created this physical body from the *dust of the ground*, and realizing that such a body would need perpetual care, a plan of health care was instituted in the Garden of Eden. The *Tree of Life* was planted in the midst of the garden. The *Tree of Knowledge of Good and Evil* was also planted there.

The plan was a simple one. As simple as making a choice. Eat the fruit of one tree and live, or eat the fruit of the other tree and die. The wrong fruit was eaten. Sickness and death came on the human race. It is not my intent to discuss the disobedience to God's command by eating the forbidden fruit. My intent is to show to all that in the beginning God had a health care plan. The fact that Adam and Eve chose to ignore God's plan and die, is no proof that a plan did not exist. Neither can the refusal of some today to recognize the teaching of divine healing destroy the truth of the matter. Adam and Eve were victims of their choice. They chose not to believe. They chose to suffer and die. Many of this generation will suffer and die, because they choose to believe those who teach against Biblical healing instead of believing the Word of God.

Healing Before The Law Of Moses

Even though God's original plan of perpetual health and life had been forfeited by Adam in the Garden of Eden, God continued to provide healing for his people. There are many instances of healing between the time of Adam's removal from the garden, and the time the Law of Moses was instituted. Not only do these healings help to answer our question—is divine healing a true bible doctrine?—there are many truths about sickness, death, and healing to be learned from them.

Abimelech (king of Gerar), his wife, and his maidservants were healed as Abraham prayed the prayer of faith for them in the twentieth chapter of the book of Genesis. This is one of the earliest examples of healing through the prayer of faith. This method would become one of the prominent methods of healing in the New Testament.

It's a very interesting story how this king, and the ladies of his household came to be sick. Abraham, with his beautiful wife Sarah, left Mamre and arrived in the land of Gerar. It is possible that famine or drought in their homeland had brought about this move.

A fear for his life gripped him as he considered the fact that he might lose his life as the men of that place saw the beauty of Sarah. They will kill me that they might have my wife, he thought. He instructed Sarah to tell them he was her brother. By doing this, she might yet be taken from him, but his life would be spared.

Abraham justified himself in this act by the fact that she was actually his half-sister. They had the same father, but did not have the same mother.

Just as Abraham had feared, Abimelech had Sarah brought to him. Then a strange thing happened. God came to Abimelech in a dream telling him that he was as a dead man because he had taken a man's wife.

This is the point where sickness enters the picture. Abimelech, his wife and his maidservants, were all stricken with a certain sickness.

Let us now consider the reason for this sickness. What was the reason or the purpose? Why did it come? The scripture tells us that this king had not come near her, so this condition could not be to punish him for an act of adultery. He had not committed adultery. He had done no wrong at this point. The purpose of this sickness was to prevent Abimelech from committing sin. As odd as it may sound, and as unusual as it may seem, this aliment was a blessing. It kept this man from a sin that would have taken his life.

As I consider this fact, I wonder in my heart if sickness, disease, and sometime even death, are allowed to keep an individual from sin and disgrace.

In this story, sickness is used as a preventative from sin and not a punishment for sin.

This healing, brought about by the prayer of faith, offered by Abraham, took place before the law and commandments were given to Moses.

Healing Under The Law Of Moses

We will now follow the flow of divine healing into the next period of the history of God dealing with humanity.

After Moses was given the law on Mount Sinai, many marvelous miracles of healing took place. Numbers, chapter twenty-one, gives the account of one of the greatest of these miracles. Many in the camp of the Israelites were deathly sick, and many had died from the terrible bite, and deadly venom of great snakes that the Bible calls fiery serpents.

These fiery serpents invaded the camp of Israel because the people, in a time of discouragement, spoke against God, and against Moses. Sin was being punished.

Healing came for them as they acknowledged their sin, repented before God and Moses, and asked Moses to pray for God to take the serpents away.

This Moses did and a plan was given to him where by the sick could be healed.

This great leader was directed to make a serpent of brass and set it up on a pole. Then the sick were instructed to look on this serpent of brass and be healed.

This is as example of healing being wrought by a simple act of faith carried out in obedience to the word of God.

Although, this is an early example of people being healed by this method, it certainly is not the last time it was used. Many other examples occur in the pages of scripture. In the earthly ministry of Christ we see this procedure used many times. A command would be given and upon obeying that command a miracle of healing or deliverance would take place.

This method is still taught and practiced today with many positive results by those who preach and teach divine healing.

Healing In The Psalms

When we think of the Psalms, David comes immediately to mind. Although he was not the only Psalmist—for there were several—he was the chief of them all. He has become known as The Sweet Psalmist of Israel.

This greatest king and songwriter of Israel was a great believer in the power of God to heal.

A child was born to David by Bathsheba. He had taken her from her husband by an act of adultery. Adultery was a sin against God in the time of David, and it remains so today.

David's punishment for this sin—which also included the sin of having her husband killed—was a terrible sickness in the life of the infant child along with some other things that would come on his family.

David lay on the earth for seven days fasting and praying for God to heal this child.

Although it was not the will of God for this child to live, this story lets us know that King David believed in healing by the power of God through prayer.

In the one hundred third Psalm, which is a great Psalm of thanksgiving, David testified in the third verse, both of the forgiving power, and the healing power of the Almighty. "Who forgiveth all thine iniquities; who healeth all thy diseases;" These words could only come from one who has personally known and experienced the power of God both to forgive and to heal.

Chapter one hundred seven, reveals to us another of

God's ways of ministering healing. "He sent His word and healed them, and delivered them from their destructions."

Healing In The Days Of The Prophets

We will now observe this great river of blessings as it flows through the ranks of humanity by way of the great prophets of old.

Elijah was a prophet of healing. During a time of sore famine in Israel, God instructed this prophet to go to a city called Zarephath to the home of a widow and her son. This widow—with a holy prompting—prepared for the man of God the last of the meal she had. It seemed that death by starvation would follow.

God had a different plan.

Because of her faith and obedience, God decreed that she would constantly have fresh meal in her barrel, and fresh oil in her cruse as long as the famine lasted. What a great faith builder!

Let this faithful widow beware. In times of great faith and victory, the enemy will seek to bring discouragement in some form or fashion. For her it was sickness in her son. The scripture says this sickness was "so sore, that there was no breath left in him." Not only was her son sick, he died! This widow, that had been so wonderfully blessed, was now so hopelessly devastated.

But wait. There is a prophet here. This prophet believes in the power of God to heal, even to the raising of the dead.

Questions began to fill the widow's mind. There was

no question or doubt in the mind of Elijah. He took the boy, carried him to the room where he was staying, prayed, stretched himself on him three times, prayed again, then carried him to his mother and said, "See, thy son liveth."

Elisha was also a prophet who practiced the ministry of healing. It was he who told Naaman to dip seven times in the Jordan River that he might be in the cleansed of leprosy.

Isaiah proclaimed the healing power of Christ, for it was he who said, "But He was wounded for our transgressions, He was bruised for our iniquities: the chastisement of our peace was upon Him; and with His stripes we are healed."

In the final book of the Old Testament, Malachi spoke of the one that was to come, saying in chapter four and verse two, "But unto you that fear my name shall the Sun of righteousness arise with healing in his wings."

From Genesis to Malachi, in every phase of human history throughout the Old Testament, we see a continual river of healing flowing. Not one time in the history of man—from Adam to Malachi—was divine healing power removed from God's plan for man. There were those—such as the infant child of David—who were not healed for one reason or other, but the fact remains that divine healing is a true bible doctrine throughout the Old Testament.

As we are about to turn our attention to the New Testament and Jesus Christ and the Apostles, I pray that faith is already arising in the hearts and lives of many as you have read of these marvelous things from the Old Testament. There are many others, such as Job and Hezekiah who experienced tremendous miracles of healing in their physical bodies.

Job not only received healing for his body, but he was also blessed with abundant material blessings when he prayed for his friends to be healed at the command of God.

King Hezekiah received healing plus fifteen years added to his life when he prayed to God, and then acted in faith by putting a lump of figs on the boil. I am sure that figs have no curative powers, but an act of faith certainly does.

God had a health care plan for those of the Old Testament, as we have now seen. We are about to see the New Testament plan for healing.

Begin now to believe, and expect a miracle.

Chapter Three

Divine Healing In The New Testament

BUT WHEN JESUS HEARD THAT, HE SAID UNTO THEM, THEY THAT BE WHOLE NEED NOT A PHYSICIAN, BUT THEY THAT ARE SICK. ~ MATTHEW 9:12

If divine healing in the Old Testament can be compared to a flowing river, then in the New Testament we shall see this river reach flood stage, flow into the sea, and become a mighty ocean.

Let's be very clear and certain on one important point. Healing is not the central theme of the New Testament. The most important teaching of the whole Bible is the salvation of the soul. Let there be no mistake or misleading in our thinking concerning this truth. The coming of Christ into this world was to provide an atoning sacrifice for our souls. To save souls from sin and Hell—through the death, burial, and resurrection of our Lord—is the dominating message of the New Testament.

If anyone reads this book seeking healing for the body, and realizes they have never come to accept, and to know Jesus Christ as their personal savior then let that one read no further until true repentance comes from their lips, and faith unto salvation arises in their heart. It is far better to be saved, and suffer physically than to enjoy complete and perfect health and be lost.

However, we see from reading and studying the four gospels, the book of Acts, the epistles, and the Revelations, that divine healing was also provided for in the atonement. "By His stripes we were healed." This blessed truth allows us to be both saved, and healed through the redemptive work of Christ. The same Christ who shed His blood for our salvation submitted Himself to the scourge, allowing His back to be beaten, to provide health and healing for our bodies.

The message to those who are both unsaved and sick is this: be saved, and then be healed.

To those who know Christ as Lord and Savior, and are suffering physically the message is this: began to stand on the Word of God, claim the promises and provision of divine healing, and by faith receive your healing.

Satan resists a person coming to know the Lord as their healer the same as he resists them coming to know Him as their savior.

Sickness came as a result of the same action that brought sin upon the human race. When Adam disobeyed the command of God in the Garden of Eden, both sin and sickness resulted.

Therefore, when an individual is healed, it is a defeat for Satan the same as when sin is forgiven. This being true—then we must conclude—that uncured sickness is a triumph for the evil one as much as unforgiven sin is a triumph.

This also rings a loud and clear message to us that the curing of sickness and disease is a victory for Christ. The same as forgiveness of sin is a victory for Christ.

Everyone agrees that Christ desires to be victorious over Satan in the sin struggle. Should we not agree also that Christ seeks to defeat Satan in the battle involving our sicknesses and our physical health?

When healing takes place in the life of a believer, it is a victory for the person. And it is also a victory for Christ over the workings of the Devil.

It is no wonder that Christ spent much time during His earthly ministry healing the sick.

Let's look at that ministry now.

Healing In The Earthly Ministry Of Christ

It would be impossible for me to tell all about the earthly healing ministry of Christ in this writing. Space and time would not allow it, and even if space and time would allow, it still could not be done, for we do not know all that was done. John, the beloved apostle, said, "And there are also many other things which Jesus did, the which, if they should be written every one, I suppose that even the world itself could not contain the books that should be written." A few examples will be cited to show types and methods used by our Lord in His healings.

Matthew chapter nine, would be a good place to begin our study. There are five great examples of wonderful healing miracles in this marvelous chapter. One of them shows the power of God conquering death, the ultimate result of sickness.

Beginning at verse twenty is the account of a woman being healed of a disease called an issue of blood that had troubled her for twelve years. This might have been some form of cancer. I don't know for sure. What I do know for sure is that she was healed. Totally and instantly. She was healed.

We are told in verse twenty-two, by Christ Himself, that her faith made her whole. For those who teach that one cannot have faith for bodily healing, this statement from the Healer proves them absolutely wrong.

This woman's faith manifested itself as she pressed her way through the crowd of people and touched the hem of His clothes. It was not easy for a woman who had been sick with a serious disease for twelve years, who no doubt was weak in her physical strength, to push past those who were much stronger than she. Her faith gave her added strength. Knowing she would be healed if she touched the clothes of Christ, she pressed through. Faith does not give up! Faith prevails! Faith get results!

Faith—put into action—was the key to this healing.

Other truths can be learned from this story. Because one has been sick for a long period of time, is no reason that one cannot be healed.

Mark, in his gospel, sheds more light on this story by telling us that this woman had, "suffered many things of many physicians, and had spent all that she had, and was nothing bettered, but rather grew worse."

When all human effort fails us, faith in God is not affected. It will still bring results.

This lady having spent all her wealth on doctors of her day—who could do her no good—was no doubt, a pauper. The disease that afflicted her shut her out from the functions of society, including the synagogue because she was unclean under the Levitical law. We do not even know her name.

This was not the case with the next example that we shall examine. Again, the fifth chapter of the book of Mark gives greater details of the story.

A little girl was taken sick. Her father—being a ruler of the synagogue—was a well thought of and a highly respected man in the community.

This reveals truth to us. Christ does not respect the persons of men. Social status or position matters not to our Lord. The pauper and the prosperous share equal ground with the healer.

We are given the name of this father. Jairus—as his name was—found no favor above that of the little woman whose name is not known. In fact, Jairus made his request first, and it was on the way to his house that Christ healed this woman.

Let not the young think that they will obtain special recognition because of their youth. Neither let the older ones think that their maturity will vault them over those who are younger and less mature. This ruler's daughter was twelve years old. This is the exact amount of years that the woman had been sick. She had suffered as long as the child had been living, and they both were healed in just a matter of a few minutes.

Upon arriving at the house, Christ heard mourning

and weeping for the child had died. This is a normal response to the death of a loved one, and especially the death of a child.

Christ said to those that wept, mourned, and made an ado in verse thirty-nine of Mark chapter five, "Why make ye this ado, and weep? The damsel is not dead, but sleepeth."

Christ does not even look upon, and view our sickness as we do. These people looked on this damsel as a hopeless case.

Christ looked on her as no more than a sleeping child that had to be awakened. Remember this truth. Your trouble is not nearly so desperate to Christ as it is to you.

This child was healed by the word of the Lord. Mark five, verse forty-one says, "And he took the damsel by the hand, and said unto her, Talitha cumi; which is, being interpreted, Damsel, I say unto thee, arise."

Do you know what happened then? She straight way arose and walked, and Jesus commanded that she be given something to eat. A well child needs something to eat!

There is healing power in the word of the Lord.

The third and fourth miracles of the ninth chapter of Matthew were the healings of two blind men. They were healed as they publicly professed faith in Christ power to heal. Having made the profession of faith, they received a touch of the Master's hand on their eyes, and went away seeing.

Then there is the loosening of the tongue of the dumb man. This was a case where the infirmity was caused by a spirit of the Devil. By casting out this spirit, Christ set the man free and he began to speak.

These are examples enough to establish the truth—without a doubt—that healing was a very important part of the ministry of Christ.

Healing In The Book Of Acts

When any great administrative or procedural change takes place, there is always a question as to whether or not things will continue as they are.

As our river of healing—that has by now reached the sea and is about to grow even larger—enters the Book of the Acts of the Apostles, we witness the ascension of Christ back to the Father, and some may wonder if this event will bring about changes in the ministry of divine healing.

There will be changes. Divine healing will not be discontinued abruptly. Neither will it be phased out. It will become greater. This great blessing will spread over a much larger geographical area, and touch a greater number of people than ever before. Neither in the Old Testament nor in the earthly, physical ministry of Christ were so many ministering healing as there are now—beginning with the book of Acts, and continuing still today.

Jesus proclaimed that this would be the case when he spoke in St. John chapter fourteen, verse twelve; "Verily, verily, I say unto you, He that believeth on me, the works that I do shall he do also; and greater works than these shall he do; because I go unto my Father."

He tells us in verse sixteen why this will be true. "And I will pray the Father, and he shall give you another

Comforter, that he may abide with you for ever;"

Then in Acts chapter one verse, eight, Christ spoke to his disciples and said, "But ye shall receive power, after that the Holy Ghost is come upon you: and ye shall be witnesses unto me both in Jerusalem, and in all Judaea, and in Samaria, and unto the uttermost part of the earth."

These were the last words spoken by our Lord before He ascended to the Father.

From the powerful words of these verses, it is evident that the ministry of Christ—including the ministry of divine healing—will not only continue, but will spread to every part of the world.

The second chapter of Acts gives the account of the coming of the other Comforter—the Holy Ghost. On the Day of Pentecost, the believers received power to carry on the ministry of Christ.

It did not take them long to get started in this activity. A great miracle of healing is recorded for us in the very next chapter.

A man who had never walked was placed everyday near the Beautiful gate of the temple to beg for handouts from those entering the temple. Surely this religious crowd would have pity and help this poor, lame, beggar.

Little did he know that two men—who had been anointed to carry on the healing ministry of Jesus Christ—were about to pass his way. Peter and John had no silver, and they had no gold, but they gave him "Such as they had," and the lame man was made whole. He then went into the temple, walking and leaping, and praising God

There are many, many miracles of healing and

deliverance recorded in the Book of Acts. It is not the purpose of this writing to list them all. The purpose is to show that divine healing is a true Bible doctrine taught in every part of God's word.

However, we should look at one more instance that is recorded in chapter fourteen. Here we find one of the healing ministers in need of a healing touch for his own body. Paul the Apostle had just ministered healing to a cripple a short time before the people of the city of Lystra stoned him. So fierce was the attack that Paul was assumed dead. The angry crowd dragged him from the city as if he had been an animal, and left him for dead. He needed a miracle! He received a miracle as the disciples gathered around him and prayed. The next day he left town with Barnabas on a preaching tour.

Healing In The Epistles

The great healing waters continued flowing after Christ's ascension. The original apostles, plus Paul carried on the ministry of signs, wonders, and miracles.

Will the church be robbed of this great blessing after the death of the apostles?

Some believe and teach that it happened that way. Miracles passed away with the apostles, they say. They never dispute the continuing ministry of salvation, yet the ministry of healing is over according to these doubters.

Both salvation and healing were provided in the atonement . As long as there is the possibility of one, there is the possibility of the other. The Epistles—which were letters written to the churches instructing then in the way they were to perform in the absence of the apostles—prove this statement to be the absolute truth.

Paul's writing to the Corinthians in First Corinthians chapter twelve list the spiritual gifts that are to operate in the church. Included in this list of nine gifts are;
- the gift of faith
- the gifts of healing
- the working of miracles.

These gifts are to operate in the church in the absence of the apostle, whether he is in another city, or whether he has passed from this life into the next.

The church of the Lord Jesus Christ—even today—is supposed to be about the Master's business of healing the sick.

We are given specific instruction by another of the great first century leaders on how the ministry of healing is to be administered by the church down through the ages of time until Jesus returns.

In the epistle which bears his name, James instructs us in chapter five and verse fourteen, "Is any sick among you? let him call for the elders of the church; and let them pray over him, anointing him with oil in the name of the Lord:"

The next verse tells us what will be the results of this action. "And the prayer of faith shall save the sick, and the Lord shall raise him up; and if he have committed sins, they shall be forgiven him." Again, we see healing and forgiveness of sin take place in the same breath. This should prove a point to all of us.

Please don't allow pessimistic doubters to rob you

of your healing blessing. Read your Bible, and know the truth.

Healing is the children's bread.

Healing In The Revelation

Our river of healing that started in the book of Genesis has become a mighty ocean as we reach the Revelation.

I have devoted several pages of this text in an effort to persuade, and confirm faith in the fact that divine healing is a true Bible doctrine. We have walked through the pages of the past, and observed this blessing. Having looked at scripture pertaining to this present time, we are aware that healing—the same as salvation—is yet real.

Now, we shall explore healing in the future. Healing in the future kingdom of God.

Do you remember the tree of life in the Garden of Eden? That wonderful tree that held all the blessings of life for Adam and Eve? Well, in the future kingdom—again—we will be in contact with the tree of life. Chapter twenty-two and verse two of this marvelous book tells us, "In the midst of the street of it, and on either side of the river, was there the tree of life, which bare twelve manner of fruits, and yielded her fruit every month: and the leaves of the tree were for the healing of the nations."

Our healing will be complete in the future kingdom. Chapter twenty-one and verse four gives us this hope, "And God shall wipe away all tears from their eyes; and there shall be no more death, neither sorrow, nor crying, neither shall there be any more pain: for the former things are passed away."

The Revelation give us a picture of perfect, perpetual healing. Never ending, but continuing for all eternity. By now everyone must surely be convinced that divine healing is a true Bible doctrine. If you are a true Bible Christian, then healing is for you.

Believe this.

Trust God, and be healed.

Divine healing—being an attribute of God—is like God Himself. No one can show a beginning or an end to either God or divine healing.

Chapter Four

Errors Being Taught On Divine Healing And Biblical Answers To Them

Jesus answered and said unto them, Ye do err, not knowing the scriptures, nor the power of God. ~ Matthew 22:9

Although this verse does not deal directly with the subject of healing, the answer is found in it to the reason many among us today do not believe, teach, and receive divine healing for their bodies. Taking in and believing the words of others—instead of searching the scriptures to know what God has to say—has robbed many of their blessing.

The word of no person should come ahead of God's word in our lives.

God's word instructs us, "God forbid: yea, let God be true, but every man a liar; as it is written."

All of the great subjects of the Bible have come under the attack of a church world that has lost sight of the glory of God. Divine healing is one such subject. Religious—as well a carnal men—have tried to eliminate this great truth from the church today. All of their efforts have failed. Their campaigns have fallen short. They have enjoyed only partial success, for though some have believed their negative reports, there are many today who still believe, and practice divine healing.

These attackers rely on falsehoods and scripture taken out of context to convince men and women to accept their thinking on the subject. They will also take the case of some individual who professed faith in God, but refused to meet God on God's terms and did not receive healing.

The saddening part of this is the fact that these false teachers are teaching their fallacies to people who need healing. For many of them divine healing by the power of God is their only hope for a cure.

Friend, don't be turned away from the very thing that you need in your life.

This chapter will list some of the most common errors being taught on this great subject of healing, and answers to these errors will be given from the scripture. Read prayerfully and carefully this chapter and allow God to speak to your heart through His word and by His spirit.

There are those who say that Jesus healed through His deity, and since men are not divine we cannot practice divine healing.

There is no truth in this statement. It will not stand when examined in light of scripture.

Jesus—although I am sure He could have—did not work miracle by and through His deity. In fact, He refused to use the power of His deity on several occasions. When tempted by Satan to do such things as turning stones into bread, and to cast Himself down from the pinnacle of the temple, He refused and defended Himself by the word of God. The same word of God that is available to each of us.

Christ also refused the use of His power of deity when He was crucified. He could have called angels to set Him free, but He did not.

If Christ did not heal through the power of His deity, then through what power did he heal? Acts chapter ten and verse thirty-eight provides the answer for us. "How God anointed Jesus of Nazareth with the Holy Ghost and with power: who went about doing good, and healing all that were oppressed of the devil; for God was with Him."

The power with which Christ healed was the Holy Ghost power. Though He came to this earth as the Son of God, His ministry of miracles did not begin until after He was baptized by John in the Jordon River, and the Spirit descended on Him like a dove.

This was the same spirit that came on the disciples on the day of Pentecost.

This brings us to the next false statement that we will discuss.

The apostles had a special anointing on them that enabled them to heal the sick. The false teachers tell us that this was only to help establish the church, but once established this special anointing was taken away.

This is totally wrong. Where in the Bible is such a thing taught? I'll tell you that you won't find such teaching in the word of God. What you will find the scripture teaching is this; all who have the Holy Ghost dwelling in them have the same spirit that the apostles had.

Peter—preaching that great sermon on the day of Pentecost after the Holy Ghost had falling on them in the upper room—exhorted that great crowd that gathered in the streets of Jerusalem to repent, be baptized, and be filled with the Holy Ghost. In verse thirty-nine of Acts chapter two, Peter said, "For the promise is unto you, and to your children, and to all that are afar off, even as many as the Lord our God shall call."

Other reasons this teaching cannot be true are these;
- If healing was to die with the original apostles, why did God set the gifts of faith, healings, and miracles in the Church?
- If healing could only be ministered by those who were present in the upper room, why did James instruct those who would read his epistle to anoint with oil, lay hands on the sick, and see them recover?

The answers to these questions are very obvious. Our God intended that the ministry of divine healing **always** be a part of His church.

Many people feel they should not ask God for healing because the sickness in their lives was put there by God. To ask God to remove something that He put into place would be a terrible mistake they feel.

This of course is not true. It is the result of unscriptural teaching.

If blindness comes from God, then every time Christ healed a blind man he was working against the Father. This, of course, is absurd. Christ came to this world to do the will of the Father. He came to heal, so healing and not sickness is God's will.

Acts chapter ten and verse thirty eight says that Christ went about "healing all that were oppressed of the Devil." This identifies Satan as the oppressor, and Christ as the healer.

In verse seventeen of James chapter one, we read, "Every good and perfect gift is from above, and cometh down from the Father of lights."

"If ye then being evil, know how to give good gifts unto your children, how much more shall your Father which is in Heaven give good things to them that ask Him?" What a convincing statement from our Lord.

Some who read this feel they are suffering for the glory of God, therefore, they should not seek healing. These same ones—who will not allow themselves to be prayed for that they might be healed—will go to doctors and take medicines to relieve their suffering. I certainly am not speaking against doctors and medicine, I thank God for our good doctors, but it is a contradiction to say we do not believe in divine healing because we must suffer for the glory of God, and then turn around and take medication to relieve our suffering.

In St. John chapter nine, is a story of a man born blind. Jesus made it plain to His questioning disciples that he would be healed for the glory of God.

Some would like to use the words of Christ when he received word that Lazarus was sick to prove that some suffer for the glory of God. When Jesus heard that, He said, "this sickness is not unto death but for the glory of

God, that the Son of God might be glorified thereby."

Continuing to read the rest of this story, we find that the sickness itself was not where He would be glorified, but in curing the sickness and delivering from the consequence of it—which was death. Jesus said to Martha in verse forty of St. John chapter eleven, standing at the tomb where her brother had lain dead for four days, "If thou wouldest believe, thou shouldest see the glory of God?" He was speaking of raising Lazarus from the dead.

Christ was glorified in Lazarus being raised from the dead. Not in his suffering and death.

But what about Paul's thorn in the flesh? Is this not a statement against divine healing? These are questions asked by those who try to prove divine healing a hoax.

Let's consider this thorn in the flesh here. We are told by Paul himself—a man who believed and practiced divine healing—that he had a thorn in the flesh. For the removal of this thorn, Paul prayed three times. The answer he received was that the thorn would not be removed, but he would be given grace to bear it.

First of all, a man who preached and practiced divine healing as Paul did would not be teaching against it. Those who say otherwise need to have their understanding opened to truth.

To help understand Paul's thorn, let us consider three things.

1. What was the thorn?
2. Where did the thorn come from?
3. What was the purpose of the thorn?

What was the thorn?

We are not told what this thorn was specifically. Whether it was a disease, or whether it was a physical handicap of some kind is not known. Some say it was a problem with his sight. Others label it something else. All that is merely speculation, because the Bible tell us nothing as to the identity of the problem.

Paul tells us it was a messenger. Whatever it was, it was there for the purpose of delivering a message to the apostle.

Where did the thorn come from?

Paul also informs us that this thorn did not come from God. The opposite was true. This thorn came from Satan to buffet the man of God.

What was the purpose of the thorn?

This problem—whatever it was—was a messenger sent from Satan to trouble this great man. God refused to remove it from him because it served a great purpose. Its presence humbled Paul, and kept him from becoming exalted above measure. He had received such a great number of visions and revelations from God, and had witnessed the manifested power of God in such a fashion until there was a temptation to become proud and exalted. This thorn help to prevent this situation which would have robbed the apostle of the power of God.

This is not an example of God withholding a good thing from one of His children, but it is rather an example of the wisdom of God working to protect His child from the temptations of evil.

Notice how Satan was allowed to work against himself. Nothing would have pleased the enemy better than to see the great apostle Paul lose the power of God, and the anointing on his life through pride and self-exaltation. The Devil sent both the temptation of exaltation, and the thorn that helped prevent it. This is a classic case of Satan working against himself, and the child of God benefiting from it.

I am sure Paul was thankful to God for God's wisdom, which exceeded his own.

With this simple explanation, it is now easy to see that Paul's thorn in the flesh cannot be legitimately used to teach an opposing view to divine healing. Those who would try to do so are—quite simply—making a terrible mistake in their evaluation of the scripture, and are doing an awful injustice to the life and ministry of Paul who preached and practiced divine healing perhaps more than any person other than Christ Himself. Not only did Paul preach and minister healing to others, he practiced it himself. This was evident on the Island of Melita where he was bitten by a poisonous snake, and no harm came to him in any way. If the life and ministry of any person proves the ministry of divine healing, Paul the apostle's does. This man's life does not discourage divine healing, but rather encourages it.

Excessive sin and iniquity in this present generation does not stop the power of God to heal, as some would contend. God's power and might is not subject to the activities of Satan and evil men. Even some fundamental Christians believe that evil dictates, dominates, and controls the availability of the power of God to this present generation.

There is not one example, in Holy Scripture that would suggest that a demon spirit can—in any way—exercise any degree of control over God or His spirit. To the contrary, there are many Biblical instances that show a complete dominance of Satan and his demons by the Lord.

If this idea of excessive sin stopping the manifesting of the power of God is disturbing you, you should consider some things from scripture.

- In the book of Genesis, the terrible sins of Sodom could not stop God from delivering Lot.
- In the book of Exodus, the hardness of Pharaoh's heart, could not stop God's deliverance from the bondage of Egypt.
- The heat of the furnace, which was heated seven times hotter than normal, could not stop the Forth Man from walking with the three Hebrew boys, and delivering them without even so much as the smell of smoke on their clothes.
- Daniel was saved from the lions in spite of an unlawful decree signed by the king of Babylon.

We are promised, by our Lord in Matthew chapter sixteen and verse eighteen that the Gates of hell will not prevail against the church that He is building.

Don't think for one moment that you have to continue to suffer because of the condition of the world. The condition of your own heart and life is what counts in your dealings with God.

There are many other errors being taught to discredit the message of divine healing but time and space will not allow for all of them to be discussed in this book. The ones spoken of here are only a small sample of the many that are being circulated among us today. As you begin to trust God for your healing, I am sure, that you will be bombarded by many, many, others. But as we have proven all those mentioned here wrong by the scripture, you can do the same with any others that may confront you.

Do not be deceived! Do not be robbed of your blessing! Let no man take from you that which is rightly yours, provided for in the atonement, and given to you by the word of God.

Let's leave this chapter with two verses of scripture that will completely disprove every anti-healing error.

Consider I Peter chapter two and verse twenty-four; "Who his own self bare our sins in his own body on the tree, that we, being dead to sins, should live unto righteousness: by whose stripes ye were healed."

And then there is Hebrews chapter thirteen and verse eight; "Jesus Christ the same yesterday, and today, and forever."

- Christ was a healer.
- Christ is a healer.
- Christ will always be a healer.

Glory be to His name.

Chapter Five

Divine Healing For The Individual Person Today

> THEN PETER OPENED HIS MOUTH, AND SAID, OF A TRUTH I PERCEIVE THAT GOD IS NO RESPECTER OF PERSONS: BUT IN EVERY NATION HE THAT FEARETH HIM, AND WORKETH RIGHTEOUSNESS, IS ACCEPTED WITH HIM. ~ ACTS 10:34-35

To know that divine healing is a true Bible doctrine and that scripture refutes every anti-divine healing argument is one thing, but to know that I—as an individual person—can be healed today is quiet another thing.

Many people have died of starvation while at the very time of their death food was in abundance in another place. Not knowing about the availability of this food, or either not being able to reach the supply, they perished. It is sad for people to die for want of food when food could have been made available to them.

The same is true with people who are sick and in need of healing. It is a sad thing to see people suffer pain and disease, not knowing that there is a healer and healing available to them.

Jesus is this healer. He is the only healer. No man can rightly claim to be a healer. Christ uses human instruments to minister and administer his healing power, but these are only instruments. Christ is the healer.

In this chapter, I will speak to you truthfully and honestly. It is not my intent to deceive anyone or to cause a false hope to arise in any hearts. Not all who read this book will be healed. I realize this very well, and I want all who read this book to know this truth.

Some of the so called *Faith Healers* would rebuke me for making such a statement as this. Their contention being that it is a faith destroying statement.

It is a statement of truth and honesty, and only the truth will "set us free." To say otherwise would be misleading and dishonest. It would be a lie, and lies do not build faith. I will give examples of some who were not healed or delivered, and reasons for this in the next chapter. However, I will show that it is God's will to heal except in cases where the sickness is a "sickness unto death."

Some are not healed even though it is God's will to heal them. Other things deny them the healing power of God. This will also be dealt with the next chapter.

The Two Extremes

As some are teaching that everyone is healed, others are teaching that no one can be healed. These are the two extremes of divine healing teaching. These are faith destroying teachings. One destroys faith the same as the other.

The preacher, or teacher that says everyone he or she prays for is healed is a liar. Secondly, he or she—while claiming to build up faith—are in reality tearing down faith. Not only is faith destroyed in the life of the one who is not healed, but also by those who observe. Of course, the one who declares that no one should expect to be healed, is a faith destroyer.

Do not be discouraged by either of these. Simply turn to the Word of God. It is God's word that inspires faith. "Faith cometh by hearing, and hearing by the word of God."

A Personal Testimony

There is no doubt that God heals individual people today. Throughout the years of my childhood—being raised in church the son of a preacher—I was witness to many wonderful healings. In twenty-six years of ministry, I have had the privilege of seeing many precious people gloriously healed by the power of God. Some of these being miracles that have taken place in my own life.

In early childhood, I was afflicted in my lungs. It seemed that Satan attacked my lungs as a child. Could it have been that he, Satan, was trying at an early age to stop me from being a preacher of the gospel of Christ? Did the Devil know what God had planned for my life? Well, I don't know so I'll not say, but this I know; everything seemed to go wrong with my lungs. Pneumonia set up on numerous occasions. An obstruction shut off the right lung for a period of time. As a result of prayer, the problem resolved as the obstruction cleared and my lung began to function again.

Then came the real shocker. X-rays and examinations by the family doctor led him to believe that I had either tuberculosis or lung cancer. He was not sure which disease it was, and prescribed further test to be performed by a lung specialist in Mobile, Ala. I was at this time still preschool age.

This, of course, was very alarming to my parents who not only made the necessary appointments and arrangements to see the specialist in Mobile, but who also began to earnestly pray to God about this matter. Not only were my parents praying, but many friends of the family were also praying on my behalf.

The appointment was secured and the trip to Mobile was made. There—after further test and examinations—it was determined that I had neither cancer nor, tuberculosis. The pneumonia and other problems had left my lungs in a much weakened state. There were also numerous scars and spots present that were showing on the X-rays. Possibly, it was these spots and scars that led the family doctor to believe that I had cancer or tuberculosis.

There is also the possibility that the family doctor was right. Perhaps God had worked a miracle of healing between the visit with him and the visit with the specialist. I will never know for sure in this life.

Even though the words of the doctor concerning cancer and tuberculosis were wonderful, there was yet more bad news to come.

If He Cries He Night Die

The good doctor then told my father and mother that a serious conditions existed. My lungs were in such a bad shape that they would not be able to stand strain or stress. So bad was this condition that my parents were told that crying could actually kill me. My lungs simply could not take the strain of crying.

It is not hard to imagine the strain this placed on my parents. To have a preschool child that was not to be allowed to cry must have been a very trying thing.

I remember well the love and devoted care of my parents during this time of my life. For this I am very grateful. I feel that I owe them a great deal.

School days were a difficult time for me and my parents. Perhaps it was the sickness that caused me to be a loner. I would rather be alone than to play with other children, so when I started to school, I had a hard time of it. Not only was I sickly, I was also a loner. I was afraid and I was lonely, so I would cry. The school would then call my parents to inform them that I had become upset. I will never forget the many days that my father came and sat with me in the school room. I am sure that he felt very much out of place sitting there in that room with a first grade teacher and class. He was willing to do it because I was his son and I needed him. He loved me enough to do everything he could for my well-being.

Thank God for the love and concern of my earthly father and mother. But how much more does our heavenly Father love us?

The years passed and my condition improved greatly.

The weaken lungs were strengthened through exercise and work. I gained weight and enjoyed life as a normal teenage boy. I gave very little thought to my lungs in those days, although I am sure my parents continued to be concerned and to pray for me.

The Call To Preach

The Lord had dealt with me at an early age, about the call to preach. In the back of my consciousness, there was a feeling that one day I would be called into the ministry. This feeling came to me at an early age and never completely left. From time to time, I would be reminded that God had a work for me to do and a call for my life. Then the call came. In the month following my eighteenth birthday, I preached my first sermon at the First Assembly of God in Ellisville, Mississippi. One year later, when I was nineteen, I became the pastor of Calvary Assembly of God in Bay Springs, Mississippi. How God blessed in that little church. But that's another story that cannot be told here.

If the lung problem was forgotten, or at least considered very little during my teen years, I was reminded of it in a very strong way as I entered into the ministry to which God had called me.

As I began to preach and to pastor, I went about it in the only way I knew how, with all my strength and might. Of course, this put a strain oh my respiratory system.

The boy of whom it was said, if he cries he might die, was now a wide open, shouting, hollering Pentecostal preacher.

This preaching reminded me of the weakened lungs. After preaching, and especially on Sunday night after preaching twice in one day, I would experience pain and shortness of breath. Though much improved over the condition of my childhood, I was aware that a problem still existed.

After approximately four years of ministry, this condition was brought into even sharper focus as I began to feel the leading of the Spirit to enter into full time evangelistic work. This would involve preaching almost every night for long, periods of time. Doubts arose as to whether or not I would be able to work in such a fashion. Would I be able to hold out to such strenuous exertion of the respiratory system? This was cause for quite a lot of concern.

Weeks and months passed. Several revival meeting were conducted, but this did not satisfy the calling of God on my life to become a full-time evangelist.

Healing Comes

God, by His spirit, continued to deal with me about this matter. By this time I had married, and God had blessed my wife and me with a fine baby boy. As a boy, I was very proud of and thankful for. Not only was I thinking of my health, I was very much mindful of the well-being of my family.

These things, plus much advice from well-meaning friends, kept me from deciding to obey the Lord to the fullest extent for a length of time. However, the call did not lessen at all. I learned firsthand that the "call of God is without repentance."

It was a Saturday night, my wife and baby were in bed asleep. I could not sleep as God was dealing with me about this thing. Arising from bed, I went into the living room of the parsonage where we were living and knelt by the couch. There my heart was poured out to God in complete submission. No longer would I resist the will of the Lord for my life. I gave it all to God on my knees that night. My health, my family, my future were placed in His hands.

What would happen, I did not know. I knew only one thing; I was going to do God's will, to the best of my ability. There could be no more holding back. The time had come to obey God.

Then it happened. As I knelt by the couch and said yes to the will of God, It happened. God completely healed my lungs and respiratory system.

Just a few weeks before my twenty third birthday, I resigned the church I was pastoring, and became a full-time evangelist.

Proof Of Healing

Preaching from two-hundred to three hundred times a year for the past twenty-one years, and traveling many thousands of miles during that time, is proof that God healed my body.

This is proof enough in itself that I was healed, but I have medical proof as well.

In the early nineteen-eighties, I was scheduled for surgery after an accident in the woods had left me with a badly broken nose. In preparation for the surgery, I was taken in for a chest x-ray.

I was a little worried about this x-ray, fearing that some of the old scar tissue might show up, and cause concern for the medical people. I knew I was healed, but I did not know if the scars had been removed, or if some of it might still be present.

Hearing the technicians whispering, as they looked at the x-ray pictures, I began to tell them that I could explain anything that look abnormal. I was thrilled at their reply. Looking at me, one of these ladies told me they saw nothing that looked like an abnormality. Then why were they whispering? This was their answer. "Mister Morris, you have the biggest set of lungs that we have ever seen in a man!" We almost didn't get them all on this x-ray!"

It Is Christ Will To Heal

I have shared this testimony to show that Christ not only can heal, but it is His will to heal individuals today.

Many will argue that it is not God's will to heal today, but there are many scriptural and testimonial proofs that prove it to be the absolute truth.

God's will to heal is revealed in the plan of redemption known as the atonement.

I believe that no doctrine should be based on one isolated verse of scripture. We are taught to compare scripture with scripture to properly understand the teachings of the Bible. Divine healing is certainly a doctrine that can be developed by comparing scripture with scripture.

Jesus said in Matthew chapter eighteen, verse sixteen, "In the mouth of two or three witnesses every word may be established." Let's consider the words of three reliable witnesses on the subject of healing as provided for in the atonement.

First, consider the words of the prophet Isaiah, he is a dependable witness. Chapter fifty-three verses, four and five; "Surely He hath borne our griefs, and carried our sorrows: yet we did esteem Him stricken, smitten of God, and afflicted. But He was wounded for our transgressions, He was bruised for our iniquities: the chastisement of our peace was upon Him; and with His stripes we are healed."

Certainly this great prophet, moved by the Spirit, saw healing as an interwoven part of the atonement. In the same passage, he spoke both of Christ's great sacrifice for our transgressions, our iniquities, and our healing.

After observing Christ casting out devils, and healing all that were sick in chapter eight verse sixteen, Matthew—one of the original twelve disciples—proclaimed in verse seventeen, "That it might be fulfilled which was spoken by Esaias the prophet saying, Himself took our infirmities, and bare our sicknesses." Another qualified witness, wouldn't you say?

The man who became known as The Apostle of Pentecost after preaching the first Pentecostal sermon on the Day of Pentecost, and seeing three-thousand souls saved, Simon Peter, clearly affirmed the fact of healing as being a part of the atonement in I. Peter chapter two verse, twenty-four. "Who in His own self bare our sins in His own body on the tree, that we, being dead to sins, should live unto righteousness; by whose stripes ye were healed."

These three highly qualified witnesses, Isaiah, Matthew, and Simon Peter, absolutely believed that healing was provided in the atonement—the same as salvation.

It is beyond me to understand how some can preach salvation by the redemptive sacrifice of Christ, and at the same time deny healing for the body when it is taught and proclaimed in many of the very same verses.

If either of these three witnesses, Isaiah, Matthew, or Simon Peter, could be interviewed on religious television or radio, or if either of them could grace the modern pulpits of today, they would teach that divine healing,— the same as salvation—is available to us today through the atoning sacrifice of The Lord Jesus Christ.

Would the religious minds of this generation have the audacity to dispute these great spiritual giants if they came in person and told these things? I think not. The puzzling thing is how can they quarrel with their teachings and writings while knowing they taught with the anointing of the Spirit and wrote under the inspiration of the Holy Ghost.

Here is the real question. Will we believe the word of some doctor of divinity, who may be more interested in fame and fortune than anything else? Or will we believe the prophets and the disciples? The way this question is answered in your heart will determine whether or not you as an individual will receive a healing touch from the Masters hand. If you believe the doubters of this day, then healing will never come to you. But if you can believe Holy men of old, you may well be on your way to a miracle.

Destroying The Works Of The Devil

Jesus Christ came to this earth in a body of flesh for the express purpose of destroying the works of the Devil.

Sin and sickness came on the world as a result of the same act of disobedience in the Garden of Eden. We all attribute the fallen spiritual nature of man, and man's need of salvation to the rebellion of Adam. We also attribute the curse of death to this same action. How is it that some teach that sin and death came as a result of the fall of man—Satan being the originator and instigator of it—and in the same breath deny that sickness is of the devil?

The truth of the matter is this. There would have been no sin or death had it not been for the tempting and enticing of man by Satan. Neither would there have be sickness.

The works of the Devil, sin, sickness, and death are what Christ came to this earth to destroy.

A woman was brought to Jesus in Luke chapter thirteen verse sixteen that had been sick for eighteen years. Listen to the words of our Lord concerning this woman; "And ought not this woman, being a daughter of Abraham, whom Satan hath bound, lo, these eighteen years, be loosed from this bond on the Sabbath day?"

As you can see here, she was bound by Satan and

loosed by Jesus.

Read again Acts chapter ten, verse thirty-eight and see that the Devil is the oppressor, and Jesus of Nazareth is the healer.

The thief (Satan) cometh not, but for to steal, and to kill, and to destroy: I (Christ) am come that they might have life, and that they might have it more abundantly. John chapter ten, verse ten. It is not only God's will that His children live, but that they enjoy life. Abundant life simply means full and enjoyable with a more than ample supply of everything that is needed, including health.

Healing Is The Children's Bread

Talking to a mother in St. Matthew chapter fifteen, Jesus sets forth this truth. Healing is the children's bread.

For as long as I can remember, we have sung that old hymn of the church which says, "Jesus has a table spread where the saints of God are fed, He invites His chosen people come and dine."

King David in his most wonderful Psalm said, "Thou preparest a table before me." I am sure that the bread of divine healing is always on the Master's table for scripture declares in Psalm chapter eighty-four verse eleven, "no good thing will He withhold from them that walk uprightly."

There are doubters and pessimist who would deny this truth and teach otherwise. Will you believe these or the great teacher? I choose to believe the words of the Lord Jesus Christ.

Christ's Words Reveal His Will

A man stricken with the awful disease leprosy, came to Jesus after He had ended the Sermon on the Mount, saying, "Lord, if thou wilt, thou canst make me clean."

This poor man—like many today—knew Jesus could, if He only would. You can, if you will. This is what the leper was saying to Christ. It's the same thing many are saying about Christ in this generation. He could, if He would.

No one in their right mind would dispute the fact of God having the power to heal. But will He use the power He possesses to heal sick bodies in our day? Some say He will. Others say He will not.

Let's get the answer straight from the mouth of the Son of God. The leper approached Christ with this important question in his mind. "If you will, you can." This was what he was saying. What was the response of the Master to this statement, which in reality, revealed the concern of this man's heart?

The reply he received was an answer to this important question. "Jesus put forth His hand, and touched him, saying "I will; be thou clean." And immediately his leprosy was cleansed." Matthew chapter eight verse, three.

The Promise Of Healing Power

When Christ ascended to the right hand of the Father, He did not take His power away, but left it with His disciples.

After the resurrection, Christ appeared to the eleven as they were eating—in mark chapter sixteen—and scolded them for their unbelief.

Having convinced them He had risen from the dead, He gave them a commission and a promise. "And He said unto them, Go ye into all the world, and preach the gospel to every creature. He that believeth and is baptized shall be saved; but he that believeth not shall be damned. And these sings shall follow them that believe; in my name shall they cast out devils; they shall speak with new tongues; they shall take up serpents; and if they drink any deadly thing, it shall not hurt them; they shall lay hands on the sick, and they shall recover."

As Christ finished giving this great commission and promise, He was "received up into heaven, and sat on the right hand of God."

What did the disciples do? Did some go back to their fishing while the rest returned to their old way of life? Did they say one to another, "Well it's over now, He's gone. There's nothing else we can do?" No! Absolutely not! Here's what they did, "And they went forth, and preached everywhere, the Lord working with them and confirming the word with signs following."

Even though Christ had ascended to the right hand of the Father, He was still working with the disciples.

The signs that were following the disciples were identical to the ones that followed Jesus. We must only read the book of Acts to see this truth.

Enough reasons and evidence have been given to establish—without a doubt—that it is the will of God to heal individuals today. I pray that everyone will be open to this great truth, and receive the blessing that is needed.

Chapter Six

Not All Are Healed

AND HE WENT OUT FROM THENCE, AND CAME INTO HIS OWN COUNTRY; AND HIS DISCIPLES FOLLOW HIM. AND HE COULD THERE DO NO MIGHTY WORK, SAVE THAT HE LAID HIS HANDS UPON A FEW SICK FOLK, AND HEALED THEM. AND HE MARVELLED BECAUSE OF THEIR UNBELIEF. AND HE WENT ROUND ABOUT THE VILLAGES, TEACHING. ~MARK 6:1,5-6

I wish this chapter did not have to be written. Along with the beloved apostle John, I can say, "Beloved, I wish above all things that thou mayest prosper and be in health, even as thy soul prospereth." III. John, verse two.

In the preceding chapter, the fact of God's will to heal was established. In this chapter, it will be shown that some are not healed even though it is God's will to heal them.

We certainly must believe that Christ went into Nazareth to work miracles and do great things just as He did in the other places where He went and ministered, but our text for this chapter reveals that this was not the case. No mighty works were done in Nazareth.

By saying that He laid hands on a few sick folk and healed them, the scripture is telling us that there were many who were not healed. The multitudes were not healed in this place as they were in many places where the Bible says He healed them all.

It was no less His will to heal in Nazareth than it was in Capernaum or any other place.

Christ surely loved these Nazarenes the same as people elsewhere. In fact, if possible, He might have loved them more because these were his own people, His own earthly kin. This was His own country.

The fact it was God's will to heal them was not enough in itself to get the job done. This fact also holds true in our day. Just because it is God's will to heal, does not mean that everyone is automatically healed. There are vast numbers of people today who could and should be healed, for it is the Lord's will to heal them. Yet, they continue to live a life plagued with sickness, suffering, and disease. How can this be?

To help us better understand why some are not healed even though it is the will of the Lord for them to be healed, let us consider another very important truth.

It is definitely God's will that all humanity be saved. He is, "not willing that any should perish, but that all should come to repentance," Peter declared. It is God's will that lost men and women be saved, yet in spite of this fact, many precious people continue on in a life of sin and rebellion against Almighty God. Just because it is God's will to save, does not automatically save them.

If a person goes around with the attitude that he or

she is lost, but if it is the Lord's will to save them, He will do so. That person will be forever lost. There is something an individual must do to be saved.

The same is true with divine healing. To simply say that one is sick, and if it is the Lords will that one will be healed, is a statement of error.

As surely as there is something a person must do to enjoy the blessing of salvation—and salvation is a far greater blessing—there is something to do to obtain healing.

In healing as in salvation, the basic requirements are ask and believe.

Many Are Not Healed Because Of Unbelief

Unbelief was the cause of people not being healed in Nazareth.

God's laws are founded on the basics of faith. Hear the words of Christ in Mark chapter eleven and verse twenty four, "Therefore I say unto you, What things soever ye desire, when ye pray, believe that ye receive them, and ye shall have them."

We are told in Hebrews chapter eleven, verse one, "Now faith is the substance of things hoped for, the evidence of things not seen."

Absence of faith robs of the good things of God.

If the farmer does not believe that the seed will come up and grow, he will leave it in the barn and starve.

This is an elementary example that illustrates the principles of faith. In the seed, the farmer can see the evidence of a bountiful harvest.

In Christ—by faith—we see the substance of salvation and healing. The evidence of our salvation and healing is seen in Christ just as the evidence of a harvest is seen in the seed by the farmer.

Failure to believe in the healing power of God, and failure to believe that God heals individuals today will cause some to remain sick.

Christ was not at fault for the lack of healing miracles in Nazareth. Neither is He at fault in our society.

Many are not healed because of unbelief. In the following chapter the subject of why faith is hindered and how to build up faith will be discussed. Here the purpose is only to show the reasons some are not healed.

Some Seek Healing For The Wrong Reasons

Our God is all knowing, and all wise. He knows even the "thought and intent of the heart." Not only does God know these things, He also knows the "end from the beginning." Knowing that some seek healing for the wrong reason and purpose, God in His infinite wisdom will not allow these to be healed.

Many prayers are not answered because they are prayed out of lust, or greed, or some other selfish reason. The apostle James, the half-brother of Jesus, tell us in his epistle, chapter four, verse three, "Ye ask, and receive not, because ye ask amiss, that ye may consume it upon your lusts." To say you ask amiss is simply saying, you ask for the wrong reason. The motive is wrong.

I heard the story of a young lady who was crippled from an injury of some sort, asking-prayer for healing that she might go to a dance. She could not dance in her crippled condition. The natural healing process would take several weeks, and she would miss the big party. Her only hope being a miracle from God, she asked a minister to pray for her. She was asking God for a miracle that she might attended this worldly function. This young lady was one of those who did not get healed. I hope she did not try to blame or accuse God.

God will not heal a drug pusher so he can resume his damnable business of selling drugs.

There are times when even those closest to Christ are denied because of a wrong spirit or motive.

Was there ever any one closer to Christ than James and John? Luke tells of an incident where Jesus rebuked them and said, "Ye know not what manner of spirit ye are of." The story, recorded in Luke chapter nine, relates how these two disciples ask Christ about calling fire down from Heaven to consume the Samaritans. These Samaritans had refused to receive the Lord and His disciples as they were on their way to Jerusalem. The disciples were offended and wanted to avenge their hurt feelings by destroying these people with fire called from Heaven. They did not get what they ask for.

Disobedience Keeps Some From Healing

Healing—the same as Salvation—is brought about by a willingness to obey the will and commandment of God. To the woman caught in the act of adultery, Jesus forgave her with the command, "Go and sin not more."

A man, in St. John chapter five, had been sick for

thirty-eight years when Jesus found him near the pool of Bethesda, in the city of Jerusalem. After a conversation with this man, Christ wonderfully healed him. Sometime later—we don't know how long—the Lord saw him in the temple and said to him, "Behold, thou art made whole: sin no more, lest a worse thing come unto thee."

Unwilling to forsake sin, some must remain sick.

A specific act of obedience is sometimes required before healing will come. A blind man once had mud put on his eyes and was told he would be healed when he washed away the mud in a certain pool.

Naaman was told to dip himself seven times in the Jordon River to be healed of leprosy. Ten lepers were told to go show themselves to the priest and offer a proper sacrifice for their healing. As they were going, they were healed.

Some refuse to obey, therefore, they are not healed. Let not these blame or accuse God.

Healing Is Sometimes Delayed

Delay is not denial. Often we tend to confuse the two. When healing is delayed, for whatever reason, it does not mean It has been denied.

The delay in receiving healing could be for a number of reasons. It would be impossible to list them all here. We will only mention a few.

Healing is often delayed while the individual wrestles with the word and commandment of God. Naaman had to be persuaded by his servants to do as the prophet had said, and dip himself in the Jordon River. Just how long the process of persuasion lasted, I don't know. If it lasted five minutes, then his healing was delayed five minutes. His cleansing from leprosy was delayed for the length of time it took him to decide to obey the command that was given to him.

When sickness is caused by a situation—such as over work or exhaustion—healing might be delayed to allow time to rest and recuperate. This, I feel, was the case with Epaphroditus as recorded in the second chapter of Philippians. It appears from reading this chapter that this man of God had been sick for a period of time. We are told by the apostle Paul, "Because for the work of Christ he was nigh unto death, not regarding his life, to supply your lack of service to me." Over work—it seems—was the cause of his illness. So possibly, his healing was delayed in order to allow time for rest. Had he been healed immediately, he would have continued his pace and perhaps suffered worse things. Possibly even death.

That the will, purpose, and glory of God might be worked, healing is sometimes delayed. If you will read the eleventh chapter of St. John's gospel, you will find the account of Lazarus being sick and dying because Christ did not come immediately to Bethany to heal him. The Lord delayed his coming for a purpose. He waited that a greater miracle than healing—resurrection from the dead—might be wrought. This being a greater miracle, God was glorified in a greater measure.

Do not stop praying and believing. Delay is not denial.

A Time To Die

Although I have been healed by the power of God of many occasions, there will come a time—if the Lord tarries His coming—when prayer for healing of this earthly body will not be answered. It will be time for me to die.

Hebrews chapter nine verse twenty-seven tells us we all have an appointment with death.

Perhaps you have prayed for a friend who was not healed. Instead, that friend departed this life. I have had this saddening experience, but it's not a time to lose faith in the healing power of God. Just because someone was prayed for and instead of being healed that one died, does not mean that our God is slack concerning His promises. There is a time to die.

According to the great apostle Paul, dying—for a child of God—is better than being healed. For he said, "To die is gain."

Chapter Seven

Receiving Divine Healing

> *IS ANY SICK AMONG YOU? LET HIM CALL FOR THE ELDERS OF THE CHURCH; AND LET THEM PRAY OVER HIM, ANOINTING HIM WITH OIL IN THE NAME OF THE LORD: AND THE PRAYER OF FAITH SHALL SAVE THE SICK, AND THE LORD SHALL RAISE HIM UP; AND IF HE HAVE COMMITTED SINS, THEY SHALL BE FORGIVEN HIM. ~ JAMES 5:14-15*

Divine healing is not some kind of hocus-pocus magic, or mind over matter phenomenon. It is not a physic reaction. It is simply God restoring health to His people by His divine, supernatural power.

By this point, after having read the preceding chapters, you— dear reader—should be ready to receive your healing touch.

Having established the fact that divine healing is a true bible doctrine, having discussed some of the erroneous doctrines being taught on the subject today, having shown that it is God's will to heal individuals today, and having revealed reasons some are not healed, I trust you are now ready to be healed. To help you attain this blessing will be the subject of this chapter.

Why Does Healing Often Seem Hard To Receive?

There are several things that can hinder and make it difficult to obtain the healing touch a body needs. The removal of these hindering factors, will prove to be an asset to those seeking a miracle in their lives.

Sin that is unrepented of, and harbored in the heart will definitely hinder in the search for healing. We are told in the book of Jeremiah chapter five, verse twenty-five, "Your iniquities have turned away these things, and your sins have withholden good things from you." If it is difficult to pray through and touch God, an examination of the heart should be made and all sin repented of. This should not be done just for the purpose of receiving healing. This should be done that the heart may be right in the sight of God.

A bad relationship with a brother or sister can stand in the way and block our blessing. Jesus gave instructions on praying through in the twenty-third and twenty-forth verses of Matthew chapter five, when He said, "Therefore if thou bring thy gift to the altar, and there rememberest that thy brother hath ought against thee; Leave there thy gift before the altar, and go thy way; first be reconciled to thy brother, and then come and offer thy gift."

We can discover from reading the third chapter of I Peter that improper treatment of, and an improper relationship with our companion will hinder our prayers.

Weak and insufficient faith can cause healing to be

unattainable or incomplete. This is not to say that it takes a great amount of faith to be healed. It does not, for Jesus said if we have faith as a grain of mustard seed we can move mountains.

Faith that is moved by circumstances—the scripture calls this wavering faith—can block the road to healing victory. People and things around us must not have an effect on our faith. Not even physical pain and suffering can be allowed to dampen our faith. Faith must be solid and steady. Faith must be anchored in the Rock—Christ Jesus—nothing else. Amos said in chapter one, verses six and seven, "Thus saith the LORD; For three transgressions of Gaza, and for four, I will not turn away the punishment thereof; because they carried away captive the whole captivity, to deliver them up to Edom: But I will send a fire on the wall of Gaza, which shall devour the palaces thereof:"

Preparations For Healing

Now, having taken a look at some things that hinder, let's look at the positive side and discover what can be done to prepare our lives to receive from God.

Let everyone who is seeking healing be sure that every sin is under the blood. A clean conscience before God is one of the greatest helps to those seeking the face of God for divine healing. It is impossible to pray in faith when a dark stain of sin is constantly before our eyes.

When Hezekiah was told he was going to die by the prophet Isaiah, he turned his face to the wall and prayed in II Kings chapter twenty, verse three, "I beseech thee, O

LORD, remember now how I have walked before thee in truth and with a perfect heart, and have done that which is good in thy sight."

This prayer coming from a clean and uncondemned heart found its way to the ear of God, and Hezekiah had fifteen years added to his life. If sin had been found in this king's life, the result of this prayer would have been quite different.

Before Jesus healed the man with palsy in the second chapter of Mark, He forgave his sins. "Thy sins be forgiven thee" were the first words spoken by the Lord to this sick man. After the sin problem was taken care of, Christ spoke again and said, "Arise, and take up thy bed, and go thy way into thine house."

Don't think for one minute that God will overlook or excuse sin. God hates sin, pure and simple.

Take care of the sin problem first as you prepare yourself for a healing miracle.

All activities that are causing sickness should be stopped. For example, no one should expect to be healed of lung cancer while continuing to smoke cigarettes.

Many voices will be heard as a person begins to seek healing. Some will be voices of discouragement. Some will be voices of confusion. Conflicting advice will come from every direction. All of these must be discounted if they do not correspond with the Word of God. The Bible instructs us to let God be true, but let every man be a liar.

Make everything right, as much as is humanly possible, with your fellow man. This may include making apologies, paying bad debts, returning things borrowed.

Whatever it takes, do it that you may be healed.

Seek to live a holy, Godly life by obeying God. "No good thing will He withhold from them that walk uprightly."

Increase faith by reading and studying the Word of God. This is the remedy for weak faith. Romans chapter ten, verse seventeen says, "So then faith cometh by hearing, and hearing by the word of God." The words of many around us will hinder faith, but the Word of God will increase faith. Read it, study it, walk it, talk it, and live it. Let it become an integral part of your very being.

Faith will permit us to praise God in advance for what we know He is going to do. There are many examples in scripture where men worshipped the Lord before asking for anything. It was so at the city of Jericho. Joshua and the people of Israel shouted while the walls were yet standing. They didn't stand long, however, for when that shout of faith went up the walls came down.

Methods Used In Healing

There is not one way or method given to us in scripture whereby individuals may obtain healing, there are several. It would be good to take a look at some of these methods now to help in attaining healing.

Asking the father for healing in the name of Jesus, is one way of being healed. Jesus declared, in John chapter sixteen, verse twenty-three, "And in that day ye shall ask me nothing. Verily, verily, I say unto you, Whatsoever ye shall ask the Father in my name, he will give it you."

What a wonderful blessing to be able to use the name

of Jesus when praying to the Father.

Talking to the Father in the name of Jesus—when done in unwavering faith—is the same as Jesus talking to the Father.

There are times when an individual is alone and unable to have someone pray for them or lay hands on them, so they must rely on this method alone, for healing.

Many have been healed by simply asking our heavenly Father for healing in the name of Jesus.

There is strength in numbers. This is a saying all have heard, and it is a true statement. The Bible tell us that one can chase a thousand, but two can chase ten thousand. By this calculation, the power of two is ten times greater than the power of one. Praying alone is wonderful if faith is strong enough to take hold of the promise, but when added strength is needed finding a brother or sister of faith to agree with in prayer will produced multiplied faith. This multiplied faith will produce results. Jesus gave us this principle of amplified faith in the nineteenth verse of the eighteenth chapter of Matthew, where He declared, "Again I say unto you, That if two of you shall agree on earth as touching any thing that they shall ask, it shall be done for them of my Father which is in heaven."

Do not hesitate to ask a brother or sister to help you pray and believe for your healing. Praying one for another often produces healing in both parties involved. James instructs in his book, chapter five, verse sixteen, "Confess your faults one to another, and pray one for another, that ye may be healed."

Job—after all his trials and afflictions—was healed

when he prayed for his friends. The brother or sister that is enlisted to help pray may very well receive a miracle also.

More faith is often needed than can be mustered praying alone so we pray by twos. Then, many times, even the amplified faith of two will need to be assisted to bring victory. We are then instructed in—what I feel to be—the main method of healing.

God has placed individuals in the church and anointed them with Holy Ghost power, that He may use them through the administration of the gifts of the Spirit, to minister healing to the sick.

This last method that will be discussed is certainly not the least, for by this means many thousands have been healed and delivered from sickness, suffering, and disease. This method may involve many people, so not only is the spiritual gifts in operation, faith that is amplified by two agreeing is now greatly magnified by the agreeing together of many.

If you have read to this point, and have followed the scriptural instructions that have been given, do not hesitate to call for the elders of the church and have them pray over you, anointing you with oil in the name of the Lord. This is the instructions given in James chapter five, verses fourteen and fifteen, "Is any sick among you? let him call for the elders of the church; and let them pray over him, anointing him with oil in the name of the Lord: And the prayer of faith shall save the sick, and the Lord shall raise him up; and if he have committed sins, they shall be forgiven him."

What Should Be Done After Being Anointed And Prayed Over

Some healings are instant. Others are not. Some are made completely whole the moment they are anointed with oil and are prayed over. For others, the healing may come in an instant sometime later, and still others will see a gradual improvement until they are completely healed. However your healing comes, give the praise—all the praise—to God.

If after being anointed and prayed for the sickness still persist, there are some things to keep in mind.

Faith must be kept up through prayer and reading God's word. Do not allow yourself to doubt. Rest in the fact that you obeyed the Word of God by calling for the elders of the church, were anointed with oil, and prayed over.

Because you have obeyed the word of the Lord, and you know that God cannot lie, it is time now to rest in His promises and begin to praise Him for your healing. It is not wrong to praise God for healing before healing actually comes.

If a trusted friend, who you knew would not lie, promised you a new automobile, though you did not know the exact day the car would be delivered, would you not get excited and thank this friend on the day the car was promised? Or would you feel that you must wait and actually see the vehicle before giving thanks? I know the answer to this question. It would be in order to give thanks the day the promise was made. In fact, if thanks and appreciation were not shown at this time, the friend might be offended.

The Word of God promised healing. We were not told what day it would arrive. We were just told it was coming. It is time now to praise God. Praise him in advance.

If after being anointed and prayed over, the Lord asks a thing of you, do it without hesitation. Your healing may hinge on your obedience in this matter. We have already mentioned the blind man whose eyes were covered with mud and his healing came as he washed—as instructed—in the pool of Siloam. Naaman the leper was healed when he dipped himself a prescribed number of times in a certain river.

After Healing Comes

After healing comes, happiness and joy abounds. This is the way it should be. However, there are a few things that should and should not be done after receiving divine healing.

First let's look at the things that should not be done. It is possible to lose a healing blessing.

It is also possible to have a worse thing come upon an individual. This happens when a person returns to a life of sinful practices after being healed by the power of God. One should never forsake sin for the purpose of being healed, and then after receiving that healing, return to sin. The Bible is very plain on this point. Read again St. John chapter five, verse fourteen where Christ instructed the man who was healed at the pool of Bethesda, "Behold, thou art made whole: sin no more, lest a worse thing come unto thee." Very plain, very simple, and easily understood. Now, it must be obeyed.

All the praise and glory for healing belongs to God. Do not try to share the glory that belongs to our God with some mortal being. It was not the Lord and some man, or the Lord and some woman that healed. It was the Lord alone.

What things should an individual do after receiving divine healing?

All the glory and praise must be given to God through public testimony. Giving open testimony to the healing power of God not only glorifies God, it also encourages faith in others who also stand in need of a healing touch. Let it be known—to the glory of God—what great things He has done.

Finding a place of service in the Kingdom of God and serving Him with all ones might is of utmost importance after being healed.

- Become a soldier in God's army.
- Lead lost souls to the savior.
- Show suffering bodies the way to the healer.
- Spread the good news.

Jesus saves. Jesus heals. Amen.

Thank you for purchasing *Ghost of Revivals Past*. If you were blessed by this book, consider leaving a review on your favorite retail site, purchasing additional books by this author at WWW.KENNETHGMORRIS.COM, or visiting the publisher's online bookstore at WWW.FILLEDBOOKS.COM.

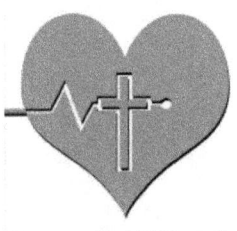

Visit our website to see our entire collection of Pentecostal books.
www.empoweredpublicationsinc.com

www.ingramcontent.com/pod-product-compliance
Lightning Source LLC
Chambersburg PA
CBHW071320040426
42444CB00009B/2057